ECHOES AND LINKS

POEMS

ALSO BY SHIRLEY GLUBKA

All the Difference: poems of unconventional motherhood

Return to a Meadow
(a novel)

Green Surprise of Passion: Writings of a Trauma Therapist
(poetry and creative prose)

Shirley Glubka

Echoes and Links

POEMS

Blade of Grass Press

Prospect, Maine

2013

Echoes and Links: poems
by Shirley Glubka
paperback

published by

Blade of Grass Press
85 Bowden Point Road
Prospect, Maine 04981-3000
bladeofgrasspress@gmail.com

Front cover painting: *Still life with books*
attributed to Jacques Bizet
courtesy of Wikimedia Commons

Back cover author photograph by Michelle Weldon

ISBN: 978-0-9666481-3-3

Acknowledgements

Five bright women—with generosity of heart, mind, and time—read and commented on these poems as they were being honed: Christina Diebold, Sonia Gernes, Virginia Holmes, Laura Levenson, and Susan Morse. My heartfelt thanks to each and all.

My gratitude also to publications in which these poems first appeared:

"Baseball and the Plated Pangolin" at *The Waldo Independent*, online, November 28, 2007

"Calendar Art Has Improved" in *Narramissic Notebook*, 2008

"Cardiac Crisis: Reversals in the Garden" in *Narramissic Notebook* 2006

"Caution before Wild Jumping Gem" in *Narramissic Notebook*, Summer 2002

"Comes the Clear and Humble Poem" at *2River View*, online, March 20, 2012

"Ever Believe" in *h.o.m.e. Words*, 2002

"Hide and Find" in *h.o.m.e. Words, 2004*

"Language Arrives" in *Narramissic Notebook*, 2004

"Notes: February, 2003" (earlier version) in *h.o.m.e. Words,* 2003

"Photograph" in *Seems*, No. 26/27

"Spell Written on Receiving Your Words about Sappho" in *h.o.m.e. Words, 2003*

"Stopped" (earlier version) in *h.o.m.e. Words, 2004*

"The Bone Goddess" at *2River View*, online, March 20, 2012

"To Try the Taste" in *The Republican Journal,* Belfast Maine, March 25, 1993

for Ginny, first reader

(of the poems, of the heart)

CONTENTS

Author's Preface—

An Insolence of Health and Joy

*This morning I was thinking about your poetry, which reminds
me of extremely fine and strong filaments of tensile steel.*
—Christina Diebold, poet and friend of the author

There are many of us: we write for decades, take extreme care,
produce good work—even work that is unique—and do not become
"known." I think of us as the invisible portion of the iceberg, the large
and necessary base. Without us no one would see those jagged
overpowering white peaks of ice, those mind-altering and suitably
famous works of poetry. This idea might not withstand the scrutiny of
a logician but metaphors, free beings that they are, are allowed to
produce irrational, even comforting, effects.

Sometimes we, the invisible, thrust ourselves upward—out of the
water, into bright air—for a moment. Here is my moment. It began
when I turned seventy. Suddenly I felt compelled to publish (finally)
my forever-worked-on novel, *Return to a Meadow*, and its companion
chapbook, *All the Difference: poems of unconventional motherhood*.
Now, a year later, come these *Echoes and Links*. It seemed necessary:
to produce a full-length book of poetry before I die. I waded through
the work of the decades. I said to myself, "Winnow and revise."

Winnow, claims my computer's dictionary, means first of all "to
blow a current of air through (grain) to remove the chaff." I had
forgotten that wonderful current of air though I remembered, very well,
what happens to the chaff. *Revise*, of course, means to look and look
and look again; and take appropriate action.

So I winnowed and revised and put the poems into order—an
achronological order both mysterious and satisfying to me, which
mattered. The result is an offering of varied styles, tones, and topics, a
mix of the lyric, the meditative, the narrative, the "accessible," and the
"difficult." I assume that what spills out here will be, in the reading of
it, different for every reader. I am unreasonably in love with this fact.

This morning I found myself reading Henry James' Preface to *The Awkward Age*. James is reviewing the work of a lifetime, preparing for a grand collection of his writing. He expected, revisiting this novel, not usually considered a major one, that perhaps it would seem unworthy of inclusion, perhaps it wasn't much good at all. Instead, he found this: "The thing carries itself to my maturer and gratified sense as with every symptom of soundness, an insolence of health and joy." Most writers won't admit to such a pleasure in their own published work but James is a wonder, a writer who unashamedly loves his own "best" finished products. And what writer, putting together a collection of her own work, doesn't at some point feel that same surprising happiness at what seems to be, after all, good enough to keep? And so very mysteriously so.

I invite you to enter, and to enjoy.

Shirley Glubka
September, 2013

THE POEMS

Write. Lie. Savor.

Four gods flapping in a square white wind.
                —line from an abandoned poem

Write the bleached sheets.
Lie about the sex and sleep they've seen.
Savor the smell when the gods are put to bed.

Keep walking the language pavement
with your slit umbrella up and open
under the clear and solid sky.
Never sew the rip.
Be eccentric. Smile.

They were white cotton,
wrinkled from being wrung.
Tiny shadows leapt, active, stringlike.
The wind was invisible, but felt.

It happens:
the square of things on a day of sufficient wind and clarity.
Steal the ecstasy.
Forego the impulse to hide it.
What use stolen goods if not celebrated?

The Madame Sits in the Soul

We find her by accident.
We find her because we need her.
She is an eruptive arrival, a black witch hat.
She is a dark dress, thick old stockinged legs.
Severe but not thin is she whose life is to wait.

We will wait with her, not breathing much.
Straight low chair against determined wall.
Blank four-sided room.

A twist of emotion slides from the corner of her mouth.
In vast surprise we watch the escaping essential beast.
She is in wild dam mode under the strict muscles of her taut neck.
The strings of her purse dance past all predicting.
She gleams in her teeth.

The Poet Speaks to the Insecure Reader

If the reach, the leap, the peculiarity—
differs—

if the word turns—
if the phrase reshapes—
if the soul rolls round, and finds itself elsewhere—

laugh!

I inhabit this intersection.
I fill it up.
Impossible, therefore, that you should also.

I see you!
Because you are not identical, not here, not now
(for I am composing, remember; composing and unknown)
and because I am not identical, not there, and not in your time,
and only because of these things,
I see.

Ah, but with only *my* eyes.

Slice though I might,
tiny is the insertion I make,
and small the view I take.

You know this—
and feel yourself so—
slightly—
seen.

Therefore, banish all readerly anxiety.

And—

if you can—
laugh.

Laugh with the muse.
Laugh even with me.

Threesome

i.

The reader is the maker:
various, ruthless, free.
The simple word lies helpless on the page.
The writer cannot save the simple word.
The writer is, let's face it, no more powerful than God.

ii.

The word is all there is.
The writer is the servant of the word.
Her mind is where it makes itself.
The reader eats the word—
if hungry—
whether it's been washed or sauced or not.
It's all she's got.

iii.

The writer is the maker.
What she gives is what the reader gets.
The word is helpless, used, served up inside the writer's recipe.
The writer is as innocent,
as daring,
as absurd as any newborn god who cooks up worlds, then naps.

The Task

Not that we know what we're doing but
seeing
(astonished)
what we've done
we keep
some—

as if a rain of seeds came
gently
or ruthlessly
never entirely inside the expected order
for seeds don't rain.

It was given
or learned
to know to hold
and choose from
those few we
with effort
happened to catch

with the hand upturned / and firmly cupped

as if seeds were drops of water
each one that minor and
slippery and
susceptible to mere
gravity.

Later
in lesser dimension
a shrunken sculptor
with a substantial seed
in a dusty studio

(thin sun from the unwashed window)
approaches the work—

a bit of carving out / yes
a bit of filling in / yes

but don't touch the center.

White Sand Is Most in Repute at Present

End the line.
End the mind.
End the world.

Begin again.
Choose an irregular element,
single sharp sand-bit,
irritating, useless
unless ground,
unless flamed to molten,
unless cooled to hard invisible substance, relative of all the gods.

Glass.
Family.
Poem.

Stop thought. Arrest it. Jail it. Try it. Sentence it.

Escaping remainder might well roam under blue sky,
under drama of great cloud,
catching small rain, iced hail, soft snowfall.

Brightly scarfed head, remember to look up. We are still here.

Something Pulled at Me

Farm smells disturbed my mother. She hated the chickens,
their dirtied eggs, shit on the floor of the coop.
Worse than that their bloodied necks, the ax in her hand.

She determined a course for herself: up the rope that dangled,
tantalizing, from clouds; the rope an immaculate
construction of words, sentences, paragraphs to be grasped
one by one, hand over hand, until, at the higher altitudes,
they became ideas; beauty, truth, being; respect.

Somewhere above the clouds: respect.

If ever the clouds end: respect.

I myself was raised as cleanly as possible,
ignorant of crop dirt and animal perversities,
a town girl in farm country.
The smells of my childhood were print smells—
paper, ink, books,
the uncontaminated dust of libraries.
Also incense, candles, clean priest smells.
Nothing, however, is perfect. On Sundays in the pew ahead of us
sat a farmer. He reeked of garlic sausage.
From Introit to Final Benediction:
my poor mother:
garlic sausage.

At eighteen I climbed into the convent
like a child coming home to bed at night.
The upper bunk, clean sheets, one blanket.
The rope of braided abstraction was firm in my hands.

At twenty-three, still wrapped and veiled, I had first sex.
Do not imagine here lust springing out,

a jack-in-the-box, a sudden exit.
Do not imagine a figure dancing free and naked
away from catechism pages, Sunday sermons,
the strict gaze of the Novice Mistress.
Do not imagine even a tired seeker emerging with satisfaction
from the final tunnel of the terrible maze of the *Summa Theologica*,
her body carried sweetly alive in her exhausted arms.

We went, avoiding boards that creaked,
down midnight halls to narrow beds
and let our long white nightgowns touch.
Some nights we kissed.
On wild and rare occasion, hands were let loose.
My sex that year was like the first thin juices of creation.
Squeezed from nothing, pale, and of uncertain flavoring,
still, it was a sort of scrawny miracle, a fact.
My sex, unlikely, inappropriate, existed.

If there was a map for going on from there, I didn't know it.
Something pulled at me,
weak as a toddler's hand with a distracted mother
and I followed with my body, half my mind,
and large unclear intentions.
We went gathering, my little sex and I,
through a stretch of rounded common coming over years,
through rough dry nights and silken places bright with red
or hushing down to pleasure blue,
through quirky growth whose brambles
rolled at last to merely texture adding interest.
We collected smells and all available varieties of touch.
We picked the fruit of language and community.
We grew a history.

Life took me to an island
and to chickens.
Yes, chickens.

Predictably, their shit was copious.
It waited, silent, under the long clothes line on laundry days.
It offered itself, apparently innocent, even generous,
to the deeply indented soles of my shoes; and stank when squashed.
I thought of the young Harriet, my mother, forced to farm.
But there was Ginny, who smells so good to me,
sitting down beside the chicken house she built
and watching by the gentle evening light
her chickens.
Over months I learned:
that there is comedy and tragedy in chicken life,
adventure, duty, pride, and social strife;
that eggs are individual,
small from a hen who lacks practice,
sometimes speckled,
sometimes such a smooth brown sculpture in the hand
that contemplation, not eating, is wanted;
that even the ridiculous chicken shape, splayed feet, pin head,
serves the eye if sunlight strikes the blue-black feathers
and a prism-split of color leaps into the air.
Then the whole brain,
held and human,
opens—
lit—
and laughs to find itself—well—*chicken-blessed.*

Assignment: Ekphrasis

> Full fathom five thy father lies;
> Of his bones are coral made;
> Those are pearls that were his eyes:
> Nothing of him that doth fade,
> But doth suffer a sea change
> Into something rich and strange.
> Sea nymphs hourly ring his knell:
>
> *Burden.*   Ding-dong.
> Hark! now I hear them—Ding-dong bell.
>   —Ariel, Shakespeare's *The Tempest*

I bring you Bubbles from the early years, *The Wire*.
We're talking television, fictional Baltimore, one very black
street resident, a skinny dirty sometimes-sober junkie.
Snitches for money, does this fellow.
Also for self-esteem, for friendship—
friendship from the murder police.
He's in his thirties or forties; maybe fifties; twenties.
Pushes a grocery cart, sells those big white t-shirts.
You remember now. Best eyes in the show.

I lay with him the night I meant to start this poem.
My worn woman body, white-skinned, bathed—his younger,
surely younger, ravaged one—imagine—
and a sure sex-hum around the rim of us—yes—
but the essence was safety, strangely velvet.
Lie us down in easy being now.
I didn't have to see those eyes to feel the pierce and thrust of spirit.

Next I contemplated Pollock, Jackson, drunk perhaps:
Full Fathom Five, early action, part still brushed,
part dripped and flung upon a set of secrets.
Layers of secrets.

I wrote:

> *The white splayed floating frog I see is not,*
> *nor winged and headless goddess,*
> *nor boot, nor Italy. Chaos of organicity, yes.*
> *And one dedicated key, butt of cigarette,*
> *nails, tacks, buttons, coins—*
> *paint-clogged detritus.*
>
> *Make shapes make meaning urges mind.*
> *But all float, all sink, all rise;*
> *down under, military father:*
> *salutes but can't be seen,*
> *staunch white surprise.*

Today a small black heart appears,
Beethoven's white face,
a skull, a plethora of penises;
anchor of orange, broken,
and shapelings pink, red, brown and purple—
little floats and colored songs inside the black-white mass of
paint lines strung upon a sea of blue-green paint.
Ungraspable, now yielding, now deceiving.

None of this is stable, or meant.
He was dripping and flinging. Following.
It took technology, x-ray vision, to uncover the white father.
Was the art that rendered the old man invisible done for the rendering,
or only to save canvas, for economy?
How is an ancestry lost and found?

I, lesbian on Medicare, happily long partnered,
have been sleeping and singing with men, some quite young.
Spinoza for philosophy.
Rilke for poetry.

Dylan for music.
Pollock.
Shakespeare with his power-wielding,
power-yielding—he's retiring—magus Prospero.
And Prospero's bright chafing flirting slave,
the lyric spirit Ariel, who gets his liberty.
And Bubbles.

Last night a torture dream: series of men,
and I the object of their efforts.
Ginny says I whimpered in my sleep—
prolonged whimpering such as Bran will do, our dog,
but he's the chaser.
I woke and pondered. The pain was missing.
Or the memory of pain.
As if I, too, survived a harmless terrifying tempest
and merely in a lyric underwent a sea change.

All this tossing, turning, dripping, flinging—
softened stringencies, attractions—
and the whole thing tilts.
No longer looking from above,
no longer flying over an extended sea of paint,
I find myself inside, upright.
Here is a slice of water organized.
The bottom is an ocean floor inhabited,
the surface is sun-strewn,
the great remainder stays between,
including, also vertical, my military man—
a ghosty harmless military man.

I write:

> I am dizzy with the ringing of the underwater bells.
> Ding dong the burden goes, all knocking on the knees.
> Ding dong, ding dong, oh, Ariel.

Before I die I'd like to drown inside some old essential
sea of laughing drunken blue-green paint,
have my knees knocked, too,
and afterward emerge,
beyond embarrassment. Amen.

Theater of Cruelty: February, 2010

> *April is the cruelest month, breeding*
> *Lilacs out of the dead land, mixing*
> *Memory and desire, stirring*
> *Dull roots with spring rain.*
> *Winter kept us warm, covering*
> *Earth in forgetful snow, feeding*
> *A little life with dried tubers.*
> *—T. S. Eliot*

I've been reading Derrida on Artaud's Theater of Cruelty:
"the affirmation / of a terrible / and, moreover, implacable necessity."
Don't worry if you haven't read Derrida on Artaud,
the point is: February is the cruelest month.

When your lover's father takes a fall
the lilacs won't even be dreaming of stirring their roots,
dull or not. They like their little underground life,
the winter routine with its permissions: to forego striving, to forget.

Then comes the tumble, and temps above normal.
All night in the ER. All life in the glare. Premature change of season.
The windshield layers itself with a constant thick wet sheen.
Rain seeps into the cellar. Dread creeps into the soul. Heaps of it.

He's only 99 and he was fine. And now he's not.
But the affirmation: "affirmation itself in its full and necessary rigor."
They want to pull us, these cruel theorists, these affirmers,
beyond the whine to willing, whipped, raw nakedness;

the mask of knowing, stripped; the featureless face, exposed.
He's innocent now of everything. Sudden infancy follows the fall.
Some days the old Victorian upright professor returns,
an intelligent nod; but that's the mask.

Familiar, that mask, a relief to see, no matter that we've
seen also behind it, glimpsed the skin of the soul,
tender and terrifying with its virtual completions,
its inevitable beginnings. Which alterations we strive to affirm.

To Fall into Intimate Slumber

We slept together.

I dreamed

> *the being of the world*
> *beyond the sacred*
> *layered the unlovely*

I dreamed

> *clear mirror*
> *bending on the verge,*
> *how it lay outdoors,*
> *making heat and light*

I dreamed

> *we watched*
> *and felt a multitude*

An oboe pulls the story
slowly twisting.
We live into the archetypal truth of years
in vast surprise
and sleep together still.

Ginny

> *If someone were to fall into intimate slumber, and slept*
> *deeply with Things—: how easily he would come*
> *to a different day, out of the mutual depth.*
> —*Rainer Maria Rilke*

In the clear mirror of our long years together
I see my early morning lover, showered, bending
to search out a shirt, a pair of pants to wear to work.
She's nude. She's on the verge of sixty. She's
shaped and lined by time, and, damn, she's lovely.
It's vigorous and individual—unexpected—
this beauty she's come into lately. Earned.

"I had an intimate relationship with that one."
She means a piece of firewood, larger, stranger
than the others; more challenging. "I remember it."
She's thinking how it lay outdoors; how she
took it to the woodshed, stacked it. It wasn't
easy but she got it in the stove just now.
It's burning well, making heat and lively light
quite like my love herself. Before we slept together—
but my soul already knew—
I dreamed she played an oboe, whole,
the sound of all the beauty and the being of the world.

In recent years, centered on the stone of duty
like a sacrifice whose ritual extends itself
beyond the sacred, separate time—whose very
length has layered on the daily, the unlovely, the
unnoticed—the music breaks, begins again, stretches
into octaves where the skew and pitch are new—and
difficult to my less knowing, less acute, less loving ear.
But lately I prefer—this is as unexpected as her recent
beauty—*prefer* this tested denser stranger music,

the changing keys, the raw disharmonies, and
resolutions that unmake themselves, abandon easy
pleasure for what's harsher, less familiar. Prefer.

And love to see her intimate with wood,
a forked odd piece of simple firewood,
a Thing whose progress over time she's watched
and felt a kinship with, as she feels kinship with
a multitude of things—things too particular, too
troublesome, perhaps too real for me. How she
takes on the world! How she wrestles with the Real
and brings it home to me! The dogs and cats and
firewood, the house forever worked on, and
the elders: everlasting fine old folk who
pull virtue from the fiber of the soul, twisting
strands together, making thread and pattern—
it's a huge, old-fashioned tapestry she's
got us *all* creating now, a mythic story slowly
woven from the long plain humble threads
that—yes—do shimmer on occasion like a new
note found, pulled from an ancient instrument,
perhaps an oboe, as in an archetypal dream.

Recognition (Work of the Lovers)

> *And turn towards my chamber, caught*
> *In the cold snows of a dream.*
> *—William Butler Yeats*

But she would bring the buried bright eye out,
the third, that sees the world.
She would prove I wasn't born without.

She would bring the buried bright eye out,
remove the residue of doubt.

From where it hides, uncertain, furled,
she would bring the buried bright eye out,
the third, that sees the world.

Diagnosed; waiting

—for Ginny, her breast cancer treatment about to begin

What if the sudden
unexpected
solidity—
dense point of self—
came into view

(this version,
like a modified kitchen,
new cupboards,
old ceiling hanging low)

as if one could decide

here I am with a
life—a
life!

I!

and didn't stop there

went on

(re-finish the windowsill,
tackle the hidden rotted places—
the places no one would ever—
you could get by—
but what if you didn't try to get by—)

went on
beyond

as if it were one's own
and of limited quantity
but unlimited quality

life
against blue sky

when strange air comes

new air
and self breathing
as if to take seriously

as if to take
with great armfuls of
strangely serious accumulation

laundry off the line
take my picture now
we are on this island only once

I am bundled with,
full with,
what is to be
folded, worn, used

from this place of years
the photo shows an unexpected
glimpse

youth
and how we were for a while
with the chickens
and the long laundry line

and never now lose

we did not know
it would come to this
armful of other

yours, mine, ours

and life still

on the mainland
in this house

with these dogs
with this cat

life
shaped inside time

threatened

held.

To Try the Taste

—*for Ginny after her mother's diagnosis*

Downward, downward she has gone
cleaving the water with her will.
The force of the dive has held
through hours and days and holy nightmares.
This is a strange tracking, without footprint
unless the mother's tennis shoe
(oh darling was it deep deep blue?)
has made a mark upon the waters
there where fair air
blew many a boat to splinter on a winter rock.

She tells her lesson over like a child.
The plainest name is Jane
if plain means unadorned and absolute.
The mother's name is Jane
who stands reliable
in spare and separate existence.
But Jane will die.
The mother, too, the same, will die.
The daughter knows the mother Jane will die.

And downward still the daughter goes
and rough above the water blows
and I have followed with held breath
and I have seen her chasing death
to try the taste, to meet the thing prepared.
But all she knows is this: her mother gone
will give her first the flavor of surprise,
a briny truant essence on the tongue,
a paradox of seasoning
as unfamiliar as an old room rearranged.

not being another

The sound of a hand-sized stone hitting dry ground
from a certain height.
—Jorie Graham

...a green thought in a green shade.
—Andrew Marvell

Slender, unrepenting women
harvesting shells by the sea.
—Victoria Theodorou

if I were another I would find it
beside the waters and lift and drop it
after ascertaining dryness of ground

and with great attention I would listen
for it is not the stone nor is it the ground
it is the sound out of which the near not-yet—

what height, though   what certainty of height
whence certainty   what ratio   and is the self
wearing green   has she not after all

turned toward the woods   walked
annihilated specificity in favor of   her green thought
in her private green shade   slender   and unrepentant

while behind her the others, those who would trouble themselves to
find the hand-sized stone, perform the experiment,
listen to real sound, harvest real shells

In the Interrogative

When in mid-February in Prospect, Maine
one crisp oak leaf, entire as it is dead,
drifts across my eye's path,
rises momentarily,
falls,
unwitnessed if not for my chance arrival,
I am compelled to inquire.

From what source such purity
over plain snow
against blue sky?

On Curved Earth

Clarity

in the sense of
transparence

I don't mean that much can be explained.

Clarity in the sense of silence.
—George Oppen

Inside the first dark cavern, which we entered unknowing,
surrounded by uncertain strong fluids, membranes, musculatures,
carried, moved, rested, nourished,
a bit of a body inside a bit more of a body which rides—
walking, talking, bending, reaching,
eating, sleeping, thinking,
rubbing, melting—
on curved earth, speck of rough ballness,
minute spinning thing uncertainly whirled inside the little galaxy
with its companion galaxies,
our little corner

       the speed and the shift—
       those suns—
       vast darknesses—

it was perhaps as strange to our former way
as entering the singularity of a black hole would be
now that we are accustomed—
space, time, matter, mind,
our lovely familiars—

or, escaping the singularity, finding the worm,
twisting with it—

or flying into—Icarus, once imagined, can't be forgotten—a sun—
our sun—
or sun of those others—

> *impossible heat—*
> *impossible light—*

or resting—yes! resting!—in a plane of vast smoothness out there.

That strange.

But in we came,
sightless, groping, sucking,
stretching and multiplying ourselves.

Susan wants to know if we are just numbers after all,
and something about the phenomenon of the counterbalance.

Christina wants sun, sun, sun
as earth darkens.

I want,
blind and groping,
writhing and panting,
stretched and multiplied,
returned to the first cavern—

want—
this strange intensity upon me—
to affirm with the poet—

> *Clarity, clarity, surely clarity is the most beautiful thing in the world,*
> *A limited, limiting clarity.*

Perhaps we are all only versions of Samson, roaring for his eyes.

Perhaps the dark cavern is mere metaphor.

The dawn comes, it has come again today.
Wondrous dawn.
But night continues to boast. It, not the dawn, is eternity.

Ah, the silver vacillations of this limited, limiting,
cherished
clarity.

Running after the One

I see you scurry—
touching, tasting, seeing, hearing—
reading, reaching—

Everything at once, you say.

Can't you see it's broken into pieces?
Can't you feel the cuts?

In the Late Afternoon, September

> *The ghosts swarm.*
> *They speak as one*
> *person. Each*
> *loves you. Each*
> *has left something*
> *undone.*
> *—Rae Armantrout*

> *Tears, idle tears, I know not what they mean.*
> *—Alfred, Lord Tennyson*

i.
Oh, don't swarm,
dear ghosty things.
You are meant to be gone.

Invisible. Inaudible. Gone.

Speak not, even in astonishing echo-drenched unity,
and kindly do not love me. Give no swarming leftover love to this soul.
Do leave behind, though, something undone.

Broken open. Sharp-toothed. Ravenous.

ii.
Over there in the sky, hanging below that single, discrete,
dark-as-lead, fray-edged cloud:
notice the chain.

Huge chain. Old roughened steel. Useless.
There it hangs.
Why?

It refuses to connect. It refuses to contain.
It sways in the slight, cold wind.
How is that possible?

Now the cloud drops a few idle tears.
All around it the blue sky continues to exist, unmoved.

iii.
Well. That was a mood.
In fact, our mother is doing quite well

and the hard blue sky is softly blanketed, completely hidden,
perhaps even resting, eyes closed.

There is currently nothing to mourn.
Look how the cat is curled on the couch,

and the dog, parallel, curves himself too,
asleep without doubt on the blue bed on the floor.

Sky Still There

Why would you enter the difficult maze
with its corners and stops, abrupt, green, rude,
unless you needed the pull of its ways

(and the sky still there, blue above, despite haze),
needed eye-level bristle, tight texture, though crude.
Why would you enter the difficult maze—

ask again, keep asking, in the nights, in the days,
for a key might be found in the change of a mood—
unless you needed the pull of its ways,

the torque, the twist into: strong gaze
from the center, hidden, god-ridden, not understood.
Why would you enter the difficult maze?

Did you need to be seen? Follow backward? Unblaze?
Return to an inchoate version? Undo? Unconclude?
Unless you needed the pull of its ways

you'd have stayed with the still eye's satisfied glaze.
The bait was confusion; and obstacles; reasons to brood.
Why *would* you enter the difficult maze
unless you needed the pull of its ways?

Over the Chasm

To follow with shorted breath
the impulse.

Having felt separate threads wind to rope,
to pull oneself,

hand over hand across the chasm,
dizzy and exhilarated,

knowing the rope's thickness / but not
how it is anchored.

Cast Away the Little Birds

I from the blue sky
bleeding limp
into silence sewn round

      (perfectly beyond my sight
      to fetch and to limit
      with the bells ringing

      to bring down from the blue
      as if mind sought in me
      flames to horizons)

beyond the fierce eyes
broken and free
talking to myself.

The Bone Goddess

Ten years she stands
stoic, silent
in this under-heated room.

If a goddess is given,
let her be spare.

I am not a goddess person,
but the bone—
the bone is another matter.

Just Home in Bed

The people who sleep with their socks on,
day is over to them, adoring and abandoned.
　　　　　　　　　　—Arielle Greenberg

I sleep with my socks on but the days fail to finish.
Nobody is abandoned.
Dreams drag them all in. Brashly bright, all of them.

How cold is the unheated upstairs room?
Is the moon up? Do tears come?

Adoration, yes. There was a time.
Insomnia and Spinoza, dear old twins, faithful.
Emerged, didn't they, one from each sock, almost warm?

Photograph

Nine empty bottles on a straight glass shelf
against a plain white wall:
pale pink, pale gray, pale blue, pale green,
round or square or squat or tall.

No need to think
who stood above a sink and drank or poured,
who held, how long ago,
what joys, what strains, how vital or how bored.

Only the clean and tinted glass remains
in camera-caught transparency—
an emptied instance, this,
a simple unsought gift / of distance.

Wanted

some thing that
wants me
when want becomes
verb effecting desire

(contagious)

making mere me

(object)

into subject
into wanter

wanter of what
spreads outward

straight-lined
elongation of
being

(simple)

the radical cut of the line
of all the lines

but of the line

into the plainest clothing
into the basic body

the cut
the cutaway

the remainder
and the divider

there lies the body
smooth as a soul

(innocent)

(afterward)

and the pieces
unnecessary as it happens

but companionable in a pile
next to essence of body

Dark Myth Left Empty

Here was, prepared against his death,
            the dark myth he left empty.
                        —Rainer Maria Rilke

If I had been Goethe I too would have left
the dark myth
empty,
fled the press of excess,
deflected the strike of paradoxical light against the
(solitary)
soul.

Of course I'm not Goethe.

Still, if she sat down next to me (Bettina)
on the plane,
her eyes aglow with prophecy and sex and unwanted adoration,
I'd bury myself in my book.

But if I had been Rilke (who himself wanted not to be loved)
I too might chide the famed poet
because a myth doesn't sit in the next seat on the plane
or jump into the lap of a bard growing old
every day.

A myth, even incarnate, eccentric, seductive, bright as Bettina,
won't take possession the way real humans do
when they exude that unwanted thing,
too much love.

So why fear a filled myth?
Doesn't it live beyond possessing?

        (spreading out whole as if already past death,

going deeply everywhere into being,
becoming part of it, from eternity—)

Still. That dark myth left empty.
I like the strict sound.
I like it as a place to leap into.

Dry

Strictly speaking, God does not love anyone.
                                    —Baruch Spinoza

We prefer moisture.
This is understandable.
Even our bones are 22% water.
Blood: 83%.

And no one these days wants a dry soul.

"Spiritual dryness" yields 63,100 Google hits.
How to avoid sere days and sere nights.
How to endure if struck by such.
Or tunnel through, emerge

as quickly as possible; at blessedness.

But what of Heraclitus?
Fire is best, said he. The drier the soul, the better.
I have always liked this radical guy.
Besides, I'm weary of salty streams leaking.

Perhaps I'm just old.

Spinoza's dry God, who doesn't gush,
who simply exists
yet can't resist incessant creativity,
burns the barriers.

Caught

If we ride the long arc, days come
when one ragged fingernail
makes the difference—
catches, clings
to what is warily other than rainbow,
more like the line between moonlight and moon,
not cool light,
not crusty matter that lacks the average gravity
(dark, dry, cold, but possessing a view).

If we hold the long arc the ride varies,
might carry and swing,
might scatter—
danger of rainbow (specific, delicate)
under naked unready limbs;
arc become mythical beast,
or meager torso
pressed flat
against huge, confident, long-muscled back,
even the bucking a pleasure.

If we ride the long arc,
days come when one silvered moment
extends to the finish,
strung taut.

Of the Many, One Is Old

foot paths—
dense woods—
all seasons—
runners with their knowing legs—
fire: kept, carried, passed—

The word hides, a heated coal,
dark, secretly combustible;
needs the skin of the old animal
or skin of the helpless, rooted tree,
birchbark, molded and sewn,
bound to the waist;
needs the running messenger.

Woods along the great Penobscot
part, courteous as a miracle,
allowing the passage,
good news or bad.

The word hides, but at the end
is given out. It might be *old*, or *song*.
It might be *here*, or *fool*, or *leap*.
It might be *dull* or *sign*; *grin*.
It might be *old*, though.

notes for the imagined, the story

—after Elizabeth Bishop's "The Man-Moth"

i.
a death that wanted to be kind,
accidentally laced like a drug
with elements of the cruel

the elementary cruel
inevitable inside the limits of love

the death planned and requested, needed

wanted on both sides like a coin
like the flip of a coin

feared and wanted by both
in this euthanasia story

which shrinks, is shrunk and shrunken

as if death were not—

let's reduce it
how important can it be
it's only death

yet how small it is
is sign, indication, demonstration, proof of
how large it is, large and large and larger

squeezed to such significance
through the tiny hole,

felt

finally

as if—

through the hole in the sky
he thinks he can climb
poor dear man-moth

(the moon is the hole in the sky)

(the poet knows the moon is not a hole)

ii.
through the hole in the story the writer wills the
death

forces the death

until, condensed,
only-death pushes through, emerges

expands

and then, please

evaporates
       like mist
            as if mist
                  mere mist

out into—

iii.
see the crocus in the yard, said Susan

the yard that
looks like a messy diaper, said Ginny
and will never be cleaned up

nevertheless, the crocus   in the messy yard

      (only a monster, half-moth, half-human,
      but a dear monster
      can climb through a hole in the sky,

      is this true?

      if you know the poem you know he falls
      scared but quite unhurt

      if you know the poem you know a tear falls,
      one tear, *pure enough to drink*)

and next the valiant daffodil, say I—

yellow as a yolk
as a sun
as silk

as if—

Grinding the Lens

> *Each creature must*
> *himself,* you were sure, *grind the lens*
> *through which he perceives the world.*
> —Frank Bidart

Must I grind my own lens?

Spinoza ground literal lenses.
Glass dust from the grinding killed him, or might have.
Prior to early death he had clear sight, hard come by.
Impossible, though, to find a satisfaction of colors,
a range of unsettling, echoing smells,
or a single dear faithful dog
in his thought.

Still, the young man could grind a fine lens.
One wants to look through it. One wants that extreme clarity
and a rest from the messier world. Passing seventy, one wants that.

To See Crimson Roses

Pull apart the

soft image

multiplying

buds

unfurling the

invisible

that flies in the night

silent

with folded wings.

Out of Nyx

Deathless gods
draw near,
wrapped in Sleep.

Death, the other,
heart of iron, pitiless as bronze,
once seized, holds fast.

And there,
all in their order,
are the sources and the ends.

Night and day greet one another
and the house holds them both
and waits until the time.

All-seeing light,
the glowing Sun
comes down and roams peacefully

and the sea's broad back
is kindly
even to the gods.

It Was a Tuesday

Crossing another suddenly disclosed origin,
I listened.

Life was better without
feigned nonchalance.

Telling the story
(strange fecundity, possibility put into traces)
my mind gathered me up,

   thought crazily,
     did not demand,
       made a decision.

The years moved in: new.

A Fertile Void in Every Hefty Tumbler

The world said to me: the glass verb is half-full,
also, each noun,
and the modifiers,
the particles, the
exclaimers –
all –
two-quarters full,
like some moons.

I smiled. This was after all amusing.
Possibly it was even
sufficient.

Decades passed.

Awe erupted.

Each shaped and sturdy word
was evidently also half-
empty!

Whereupon came the impulse to dance extravagantly
under the faint daytime moon,
anticipating night.

If Leaves Were Language, Dry, Fallen, and Perfect

Jump! Jump from the back of the wagon
into the heapings of leaves.
Dry! Crisp! Remember the smell?

Roll around, little souls.
Roll around and laugh with your cousins
into the early dark, under reliable stars.

Tomorrow: tomorrow we speak.

Another Umbrella Poem

Here is the color into which all others escape.
Open it, like an umbrella. Hold it firmly over your head.

Is there a slit in the silk next to that rib?
Never in rain, then; good enough for the glare of sun.

Walk on the cultivated path in the leisurely old English novel.
Wear your long proper no-color skirts.

They are not entirely clean.
This fact and the slit give you away.

Your umbrella's imprudent catchall essence is also scandalous.
Sit down on the new-mown grass, might as well.

Forego protection from staining, from insects.
You're a tough one, aren't you? Tougher than you meant to be.

But the umbrella bursts.
        The inclusive escape is reversed.
            Insisting, singing, leaping forth—
                proliferation of the variegated world!

To the Man Who Wrote the Poem on the Internet Today

There's me and there must be two others, don't ya think?
Let's say so. All right, then.
Sir: we three heretics aim at your suffering mind
this particular literary morning
several rough blasts of educated joy,
never mind how unwelcome.
Flat-out whitegold rushing gladness
comin' at you from that angsty sky, mister.
Halleluia glory in deep carmine, too.
Triadic silly giggles, clarion green,
cascade upon your day. They're for good measure.
Open your goddamn heart, sonny. This ain't no time for mush.

Three Words and Two Deaths

i.

I would like to oppose—to each other—the first two words:
red, miasma.

Red is the word of the child, the round ball bouncing, vivid,
going somewhere.

But the car, the poor dull gray car, comes in slow motion
down the dream road,

rolls by, defying time, excising the child.
Not my child. Any other mother's child, any father's,

child of the village,
somewhere there is a village.

Watched or unwatched,
the child with the red shirt chases the red ball.

This is nightmare, with dusty brown road,
glare of the sun.

The driver is a child herself, learning and murdering,
and the second word is *miasma.*

Words come from nowhere, arriving like the car.
Red. Miasma.

Or out of the communal psyche.
Not from nowhere, then.

I await the third.
There will be a third word.

The miasma meanwhile is not vivid, is going nowhere,
is vague, unwanted.

No one chases a bouncing miasma, craving it,
ignoring oncoming innocent danger.

Perhaps if the very soul contracted,
rolled itself into itself,

became firm (but still angle-free) form,
a specific, a sphere—

if it turned red, vivid—
a holy ball, bouncing, going somewhere—

and after it will run, laughing,
a red-shirted—yes?—

But what child wants to play with a concentrated miasma,
even a round red one?

(I await the third word.)
(The third word has not come.)

ii.
The third word has come: it is *down*.
It is plural, and young, and old,

a matter of fine fluffy feathers, soft.
Down is the first covering of the baby bird.

Down also hides, an insulating layer,
under the contour feathers of an old bird.

Even the toughest old red bird has some downy red fluff, then,
under the feathers that give shape and enable flight.

Every old bird of any faded color must have—
don't we insist on this?—

a touch of soft red—downy—
layered into the miasma of the old bird soul.

iii.
Look! The soul is well-rolled now and here comes the child after all,
the red-shirted child,

a giggling little ghost of a child,
and she reaches out.

Around the old bird soul with its tucked-away red
(which only a ghost child can see),

she puts her fat little hands,
gently.

Art of Accident

—for S. B. Sowbel

Look at the photo taken after the accident:
back home, stitched like a loved worn doll,
right up the forehead, stitches making a new

hairline, how beautiful she is with bright rosy
bruises under both eyes, slack lips only
slightly paler, pink without lipstick, the woman

is a color witch, saturated red scarf wrapping
her neck, wild huge red and green art,
hers, hanging here and here on walls behind

the very, very close-up caught stunned open
absent- or inward-eyed privacy of the whole
human face and how lovely the soft blue and

black plaid of the soft bathrobe with its soft
folds, we get only a glimpse but we
want to wear it before we dress for the

next accident-free day of the lives we
expect, friend-filled, enemy-spiced, as
if existence will never spin its

wheels on ice, mud-disguised, and
plunge and roll over an 8-foot embankment
into a brook, not our existence, of course not,

we're the ones through whom the lucky
energies of life are streamed onto the precarious
existence of all those others, are we not.

Goose Boustrophedon

—after the painting by S. B. Sowbel

> boustrophedon: the writing of alternate lines in opposite directions, one line from left to right and the next from right to left. Some Etruscan texts are written in boustrophedon style, as are some Greek ones of about the 6th century B.C. The word is from the Greek *boustrophēdon*, meaning literally "to turn like oxen" (in plowing).
>
> *—Encyclopedia Britannica*

The unseen ox as large as the field
pulls the plow, reverses direction,
repeats, reversing, row after row.
Over the field as large as itself,
with determined vision, painted, repainted,
the unseen ox pulls the plow
and the furrows are readied for unseen seeds.

It is not easily given from the soul to the self
to remember the unseen ox and the field unseen
but the paint which disguises also enables.

Blood-red the milk that drips from the uplifted bill of the goose.
The goose of the gods that has entered the sex.
The sex of the universe, lit by the vaginal flame.
And the person, the parallel, reaching and green.
And the ox unseen, plowing, repeating.
And the writing invisible, dense and ancient with strangeness.
And the woman, the artist, caught by complexity, paints this.

Dog in Chair

—*after Francis Bacon's "Painting" (1946)*

Our Emily is upside down.
She's flung and twisted and asleep,
her belly exposed,
her hair a whipped mixture of black, white, and brown,
a hurricane, stilled,
captured by camera.
One leg extends straight against gravity,
another mimics a faggot's wrist.
Imagine those perfect teeth painted by Bacon, both rows.

They'd glow white like the light-struck chin
of the seated man
under the black umbrella
in front of the crucified steer;
or like the layer of fat
around the raw meat
near his black-clad knee.

That pure black.
That raw pink.
Those necessary, violent patches of white.

Before it was an umbrella, a crucified steer, man and meat,
it was only a bird trying to land.
Then came catastrophe.
The man's head is half-hid but his teeth show.
They are white like Emily's, and beautiful.
They, too, might be innocent.

Emblem of Appetite

Imperatives

       spreading

              cold black pressure

need their prey caught / reflecting / unending.

Stagecraft in Red (Justice)

Heavy scales hang with a truncated sword.
A young girl plays her part:
seated, enthroned, stuck on a card.

Her vestment is vertical.
Her coif is tight.
Her crown is stiff.

She is subject to us, a spring bud of justice,
a rose not yet thick of thorn.
She claws her own tender knee.

Circles abound:
firm circles, surrounding the scene.
They lack the third dimension. They lack the fourth.

A bloated ghost fumes under her soft foot.

Ever Believe (October 15, 2001)

> *Did anyone ever believe that the dead woman*
> *they buried with a bone needle in her hand*
> *would use it to sew a new jerkin in the country*
> *beyond the moon? Or that the young man whose*
> *mutilated corpse they placed on a shield would*
> *use it to defend himself? No, our ancestors*
> *were not so simple. They did these things*
> *without expectation. They did them in despair.*
> —Hayden Carruth

They did them in despair. Well, that's true, too. Let it all mix.
Shine will sneak around the phosphorescent edge, emit and pulsate.
All clarity via contrast. Or not.

Done deadness. The cooked and the eaten. Elements exeunt.
It's so old. We walk on them, dance on them, fuck for fun on them,
crude, undeveloped; kill upon the carbonized remains,
then shed a shining tear and smile sadly,
so young are we still.

Wartime. This round, it's al Qaeda, the terrible Taliban.
Not of course Afghanistan unless you happen to be there and
notice that bombs not quite aimed your way manage to
kill you despite. Nobody's perfect, we say, we who—
it's me too this time, it's not Them, inane Others,
I'm in there pulling the lever or maybe it's
pushing the button right-clicking the mouse what do I know
I'm in the cockpit but blind uninformed as to detail
forgot to read the manual never did make it out of bed
find the class on how to get those bombs to leave me
take their target—complain if a bit of fear forms on the
morning tongue and we have to use extra
mouthwash before the real day starts
so no-one smells us.

I'll tell you why it's Me Too this time. I'm forked.
Female and nearing sixty I won't be forced to fight now will I?
But all my strands are braided and don't get
combed out come nighttime anymore.
Each hair carries on its carefully curved twined twinned path
some particle of—Mr. Bush, say—
as well as the woman under the burka who might just
cheer while she trembles, dance while she dodges,
what do I know, old peacenik, old dyke that I am,
amazed at how we all got put together with such skill,
and this is just one head, mine,
on which dance, fuck, kill a multitudinous tiny
(but not tiny to them) set of folks I can't see,
other worlds don't you know, with, maybe, their own sunrise,
shine of the dew on the grass early mornings in mist,
that sort of thing, all beyond my ken of course,
all beyond my ken.

Notes: February, 2003

Sent rice to the President, one-half cup.
If your enemy is hungry, feed him.

Signed our names, wondered if the ziplock bag would hold,
imagined the screeners, *What's with all this fucking rice?*

Thought they might fear it was anthrax-laced,
almost wanted them to, but they're just people.

Perhaps they said *Rice!* and enjoyed work that day.

The cold dry of this long white winter holds.
Temps near zero, with wind; days stacked flat.

Newspapers wait for recycling in the unheated hall.
The rice won't get to Iraq, no hope of that.

Poetry muscles weak as Danby,
cat with superior chi, laid low by a faulty thyroid.

Chewing her kibbles today, pulse one-twenty and strong.
But she's so thin, her skin a loose wrapping for bones.

Keep seeing a white empty box, keep feeling a blank solitude.

From Under

Like the dank cellar in unyielding wetness of weather,
its walls seeping, its brown flood,

so the soul with what falls from above
and what oozes from its own ground.

Clear bright air seems a midnight dream.

Small Poem after Reading Blake's "Milton"

How to rise from the couch,
emerge from the terrible comfortable void,
the void that is the womb from which, perhaps,
some next thing will come?

If the chiding vision hides, how?

Visitor at Day's End

The thought comes,
limping, weakened, past its prime.
Here, sit, say I.

We settle ourselves,
catch our respective breaths,
give each other the eye.

You knew me long ago,
why the extreme delay, I ask,
embarrassed by my

irritation and this
absence of tea and cookies,
this difficulty seeing past the cane.

We're on the old front porch on Seventh Street,
two rockers and twilight and—
I wish he'd make his meaning plain.

We sit with nothing to sip.
The neighbor architect comes home from work.
The moon is on the wane.

Untitled American Haiku

Water bucket ice melt,
sun-struck, shining
over last year's sparrow.

Yield

The human mind repeats itself.
Mere memory cannot prevent
unwanted repetition which
is woven in the larger web:
stern stars keeping to their single
constellations; the steady shift
of seasons; difference in the skies,
repeated; collisions in the
cosmos, ungentle and unlearned;
the unexpected bright remains.

If Not for This

If not for this time on the floor,
this stretching of a stressed muscle,
this room's window,
this wide sky,
these white clouds more substantial than they look,

the subtle, exact, clear
amplitude between stitch and design,
between ache and release,
where infinity and eternity abide,
would not reveal itself.

What happens next is harsh.
Suffering, not only my own,
becomes acceptable
and simultaneous to joy
in this wrong, or bifurcated, or saved,
or surprised simple bright rinsed: heart.

Cardiac Crisis: Reversals in the Garden

Like the Victorian lady she most definitely isn't,
my mother, it appears, has now "a heart."
I, distant, sit to type as she is driven,
in all senses, to the cardiologist.

My own free mind cannot hurt my mother
is the line I write. What happens when a
hint of wisdom like a snake surprised
darts out its tongue? Do I stay, make

my eye meet its eye, or run? I could, coy,
stop there; right there in the middle, half-line
left dangling. Or tell: take the liberated
moment, burnish it against my own rough cloth;

in a special pocket sewn from syllables,
hide it; hoard it; love it; tell you, reader, how I love it.
Tell, too, about the twists of innocence
inside that other love, that much-revised,

erased and written-over, ink-stained, crumpled—
flattened, ironed, saved—
reread—she is my other half-line now,
left dangling.

Caution before Wild Jumping Gem

—for my mother, Mother's Day, 2002

To put into the urn of the language
this complex thing,
gift of being,

tangle and turn of it,
wriggle and flight of it—

> (center calm as a pool
> with liquid light,
> with jeweled hues,
> sacred and reliable)

impossible

absurd

necessary

Calendar Art Has Improved

This month a lone small
grasshopper sparrow
open-mouthed on a wide sand dune.

Straw-toned, apparently dry, this
simple dune. Stands, this simple
bird, on one spent upright stalk—

the stalks are all upright
with sky behind, dark threat—
but lit, stalk-and-bird, lit

from a subtle unseen source,
one spread ray, left over, offering
(plain-feathered, hint of the scraggly)

essence of the unexceptional.
Out pours the tiny song, insect-like,
dry, bare, and brave. Out spreads

the wide dark sky behind. Down
sink I to stretch a set of muscles
on the cold and steady floor.

Out of the Violin

"What seems so far from you is most your own."
                                    —*Rainer Maria Rilke*

I almost feel it, impossible to think it. How it escapes,
how it surges, a wave upon a one, leaving, arriving.
The absolute present of sound, the entire absence.
Even the echo an absence. Do some minds *hold*

unbodied notes? Out of the violin—body, string,
bridge and bow—this mediate source quite physical—
and from a dead man's mind—
and from a young woman's hand, arm, brain, and silver soul—

Because I have the luck—
impaired or shrunken / bits of brain—
memory of music has a hard time forming in me, staying.
Surprise repeats itself.

What if I knew the next note, the switch, the intrusion,
the way the clash is coming, the route through? What if
I could foresee the assault, beauty bearing down,
extreme essence of a single note held high, and for so long?

Tension

I count five

       light breaks

growing closer

       and yet less

is not quite

       is / and means

As the Field Is Revealed

—*after Ellen Goldsmith's "Before the Curtain"*

The great gap
stretching from soul to sight
shall be lit;
the thing itself,
though at present encased
like body and blind head
inside muscle, inside bone,
shall be sudden seen

unless revelation
smear the wet ink,
one large hand
swipe the page,
douse the light,
and deep night take all.

For All My Cherished Suicides

Black lake, black boat, two black, cut-paper people.
—Sylvia Plath

I forgive you everything and there is nothing to forgive.
—Gertrude Stein

I must be standing on land. Perhaps it's even daytime for me.
They, cut-out humans in their black boat on their black lake,
crossing the waters of essential night, are far from me, safely clear.

Don't you safely see them, clear despite pervasive dark?
It's only a mythic image, nothing to do with now,
bits of thick paper cut by a child, two-dimensional.

Isn't it?
Oh, Sylvia! I forgive you everything and
there is indeed nothing to forgive.

Dear Gertrude, please understand the rest of us. Lacking genius,
we nevertheless appreciate your lines. This one is a good one,
it lets us stand everywhere at once. We like that.

Time and Again

> *We come too late for the gods*
> *and too early for Being.*
> *—Martin Heidegger*

So many gods to choose from and
all of them dead and I am indifferent

but not to my own
under moss, under rock, behind cloud,

still as a struck mouse inside an old clock,
or disguised as the tick-tock itself,

the seconds divided and multiplied,
explosive concoction of quotient and product,

remnant night-seen, in daylight disguised,
refuses to stop. But it's I, only I, refusing to stop.

Philosophy with Small Shine

To sing/zing/sting/wing
with the particularity of
one's own speck-like
unfinished
existence

one's singular in the
happenstance of
time/place/grid

simple ratio and
plenitude

(shine here)

one grain ego
to near-infinity of
Other/others

determinedly
pleasant

(today)

under rain
coming down with—

listen—
gentle *irregular* rhythms—
small, wet—

and with
no promise.

Amor Fati: Poet Approaching 68

To capture,
aptly to caption—
how many years reaching for that?

Realize.
This happened, or is happening. This.
Strive, walking up the path overgrown with specifics, to *realize.*

In your life, this event. *Don't you realize?*
Accusing the self of vagaries
of avoidance

as if sufficient effort
and enough
language

might define, fix, set—

like branches outlined by light;

as if you still sat on the old worn porch on Seventh Street,
late winter afternoons, Winona, Minnesota,
you, adolescent,

and still named
repeatedly
one preference:

black trees bare against sky.

But it all ran wild in the older years.
Why clip it back?
This —*experience*—escapes.

Even on a Maine day in March,
weather hovering between mist and rain,
irritations thriving in the household,

why long for the clear light of definition,
the firm full grip of the heart,
of the mind,

the shining beat of being itself
caged like a bird with
a clear call,

a bird that cannot squeeze out through silver bars,
its existence so robust, so satisfied—
But that's not what I meant to say.

I was lying in bed, awake, my net spread, the trap set.
I could hear it breathing, the thought
that wanted not to be caught.

Moonlight, enough of it now.
Silence, except for the lap of the coming tide
and my own breath, my own beating heart.

It came close, its sudden fur sleek and silvered,
its feral nature out of place amid my tame particulars.
Imagined. It was only imagined.

By morning, though, it seemed possible,
made of something beyond
moonlight, shadow, quick movement.

It seemed near, and asking. It laughed at the trap,
played in the net, wore it for decoration,
ripped it and stepped out.

Such delicate grace in its great soft paws as it took those first steps!

You'll never catch me, it said,
tossing the words over its shoulder as it calmly departed,
but put me in a poem and be glad.

Hide and Find

On the way to the lost word

when you disguise yourself
by blending excessively
in order not to get shot

via fatigue
or its plural, fatigue's plural

squatting behind a bush—
khaki and green,
dark brown and black—

this is not my life,
this is so far from my life.

The brain has brakes on it / breaks in it.
The word for the disguise / hides.

Tomorrow it will rise up
and step out of the hole it hid in,
recognizable as a table,
as silverware,
as a dish drainer,
the kitchen persisting,
unlosable, loved.

Claustrophobia,
but that's not the word.

How difficult to wait for revelation
when it's right
there
and only some

off-slant
of an
electrochemical
event
results in the

camouflage.

Stopped

Sometimes the tangle:
rag around a stick,
dirt-gray, damp,
on this,
my day-dark path,

so humble,
so obscure,
it rouses wrath.

Who came here?
And did what deed with it?

Rage at what is fragile,
rage at rot,
the held tongue of the thing,
how it won't talk,
will not reveal its origins,
will balk at my demand

that clarity and hot connection
to the web of things
be here
this instant
on this path

in this poor rag
which, after all, look closer,
wants to beg a pardon,
would open its slit mouth,
revere my need,

but can't.

A foot away
the claim of trillium,
the confidence,
brings shame.

Goldilocks and the Basket of Language

Ho, she's carrying it through the woods, she must be a very big girl
and we know she's threatened,
we know she'll be
deceived.

But what strong arms and even the hint of her white apron is so
reassuring,
how young can she be, not young enough to
worry over—
not if she, like a goddess,
can lift such a basket and skip along singing with her large lungs, la la.

Or is she under that hood secretly terrified by her task?
No, I think she's oblivious and knows more than we do.

Look!
She's throwing back the red hood, it falls over her generous shoulders.
She's definitely goddess-sized and here she is at our door.
She rings the bell and offers it—the basket—
she's uncovering it—

off comes the bright white cloth
with its squares crisp from the folding—

> it lay on the shelf for many a long silent year,
> white cloth folded,

> then was taken down,
> opened and placed,
> a careful white cover—

> now it flies off,
> a departure—

all of which makes us, door-answerers, into the big bad wolf
disguised as Granny
and evil and
hungry—

or maybe just curious because, look, she's unpacking the basket,
it's one of those miracles—

loaves and fishes   *oil for the lamps*   *no bottom to the basket*

Don't just stand there, darlin', invite the girl *in.*

Blades Cutting Upward through Density toward Sky

> *"What we* like *determines what we are..."*
> —*John Ruskin*

> *"I like the look of a mountain of matter."*
> —*Fanny Howe*

I went back to look for myself.
Not there. Brush and tangle and
heaped multifarious event. But not there.

It had been years, perhaps decades.
Accumulation was evident.
Obfuscation, expected, did not reveal itself.

Today I sat until I saw. Tiny shoots of clarity.
Do they grow in the soil of such
mountains of matter? Are they loved?

Baseball and the Plated Pangolin

I don't much care about baseball,
or pangolins.
I'm no Marianne Moore.

But this morning
NPR gave snippets of a recording
long lost, now found
in a box
in a dead man's garage.

Young Sandy Koufax pitched a no-hitter.
The crowd went wild, as expected.
No surge in me there.
But the teammates leaped over each other
just to touch him—

I was on the floor
stretching against pain,
managing the older body,
far from the field.
Spring sun warmed the rug.

They leaped
and reached my solitary heart.
Surprised by tears,
I thought,
Oh. I thought that. *Oh*.

I meant
So this is it,
we leap and touch.

As if to grasp: a definition

At last, this terrible clarity,
this compression—

as if we do / repeatedly
conceive each other—

you, all of you, carrying me,
I, in my entirety, carrying you / each of you.

Each birth is virgin
and difficult.

By difficulty we are distilled.

To take a sharp / hard joy in sheer existence—
as if it were possible now—
to grasp—

as if it were a piece of sculptured / burnished
steel in the hand—
as if it were
a talisman—

Spell Written on Receiving Your Words about Sappho

—for Zarod, on her 60th Birthday

Sit.
Sit with the bright, with the old.
Sit with chips of her poems that wait in your lap.
Sit knowing her loving and wildness, her long ago pain.
Sit, taking into your hands half-lines once sung whole.
Sit on rock, sit beside ocean, sit in sweet chair, warm with sun.
Sit in center that radiates lines, leaps outward, rushes home, hovers.
Sit holding the long string of time, the linear wonder.
Sit and be. Be reader, be lesbian, broken and strong with the years.
Be one who feels her way back along layers,
gets cut on the fragment's spare edge, cut into.
Still, after years, be ready. Be incomplete.
Fling against, laugh into, leap over time.
Take history into arms that are practiced. Wrestle and cherish.
Crunchy as rhubarb from old, gnarly root, come. Come home.
Hooting down canyon, carry echoes in backpack, blue-tuned.
Clear as a freshet, ready for deep ancient sea, dare to enter.
Find fragments buried, hard, hinting, yours. Find Sappho.
Find next decade. Find seventh. Find luckiest.
Magic pierce and suffuse you. Magic upthrust wonder,
upthrust wisdom. Magic and echo of Sappho be yours.
Be newborn and well worn. Be all.

Near a White Rabbit

Notice how
windows
are quiet now.

Moons floated up,
became,
and so escaped.

In such a sky, I think of children.

The Work

...this werk asketh a ful greet restfulnes...
                                    —*Cloud of Unknowing*

Rested, then. Ready.
The usual eyes are closed, covered, protected. The others—

or perhaps only one other—
the famed third—

but more likely many, facing all possible—
an infinity of eyes, monstrous infinity—

are being prepared, peeled—
the rinds of eyes curling into the steel sink—

the skilled hand, the paring knife—
time to fly back to where they keep your skin—

But stay.
Next comes God.

Lines

Lines straight as light, you have seen light,
seen it escaping the cloud's edge,
reaching.

Lines like that, all the way to your own eternity and
not always invisible. The proper cloud,
the specific slant, renders them—
offerings—
visible. Even the human eye then sees.

Ignore shame at the leavings of the former self;
bypass, delete.
Delete not the leavings but the shame.
Shame will break and tangle the lines,
knot them wrongly, distort the design.

As for the leavings:
find a tender half-smile for them,
left in the path as they are.
Stop, stoop, pick up.
See how contained,
how definite,
each moment a shy self.
Put it down carefully.
Carefully do not step on it.

Turn next to the straight line, longed-for,
claimed. The line to your own
eternity. See the fine, thin, available
reach of it, outward, inward,
how it remains and escapes,
how it freshens itself,
how patient it has been.

Forms of Us

—in memory of Barbara McCarthy

behind windows

    an infinity of echoes

the wind will hold

    every moment / still / in moving air

Meditation Opposing Flight

> *The point of the nail is applied to the very center of the soul*
> *and its head is the whole of necessity*
> *throughout all space and time.*
> *—Simone Weil*

> *at the nail's point the hammer-blow*
> *undiminished*
> *—George Oppen*

I have seen in my mind's eye the great nail that pierces the soul:
clean, new, shining with light.
I have imagined a thrifty motion of a distant god,
a hammer striking straight.
The pinning against premature flight would be precise, perfect.

But perhaps it's a rusty nail,
or bent.

No matter.
Let the prayer rise.

Nail me to this grid—
swiftly, thriftily—
before I—
inadvertent—
fly.

This is a prayer to an unknown deity,
a god too near for perspective,
too far for presumption.

Prayer against flight,
prayer to be held,
nailed to the weather-worn board.

Prayer for a god's efficiency,
thrift,
spare use of illimitable powers.

Prayer, then, born of hubris,
offered despite:

Nail me swiftly, thriftily,
before I fly.

Complications of Desire

If we throw far the human net out over the night sky's ocean
and wait as it rises against all gravity—

aware how silly, how frivolous such fishing is—
laughing and hopeless, but pulling ourselves upright again

after each bent capture by the gut-cramping fit of giggles,
after each humbling impossible roll in the field of snow

(for it is never Spring when this happens, it is never not cold,
never far from that feeling—the last hurried winter moment

before the inevitable call to supper when we will have to break away,
leave the delicious dark, the good sharp sting of the wind,

leave the wild running and all of us tumbling into a pile
as if we were a single snowy animal, breathless and triumphant)

and stand again, and upward again cast the determined glance
at the flung net rising in the night, holes widening,

strings stretching, fraying, their knotted beauty, their firm pattern
in definite jeopardy, we do know: nothing can be thus caught.

Into the house we go. We climb the stairs.
We enter the room with the desk.

No longer the mythical night,
no longer the childhood winter dusk.

Return to daylight. Work.
But they flee from us that sometime did us seek.

All the little sentences are escaping,

their bright backsides catching the slant rays.

Nevertheless we sit,
letting the late sun weaken.

If we turn on the standing lamp, if we open the book,
what will we find?

Only what was long ago gathered into the sack of the soul:
Nothing is so mute / as a god's mouth.

What shall we ask now?
What shall we want?

Comes the Clear and Humble Poem

Daily the difficult, the inexplicable, the gift.

Grit to transparency ground,
deeply tinted, heated,
carefully cooled,
broken.

Pieces then, fitted and placed,
based.

Lead seals the treacherous,
the accidental / edges.

Torque

Singularity: point at which a function receives an infinite value,
especially when matter is infinitely dense,
as at the center of a black hole.

Singularity: point in the future beyond which
overwhelming changes make reliable predictions impossible.

Time twists.
Shape is shifted spaceless.

At the root of the whirl of shape and order,
at the base of the time/space phenomenon,
deep in the core—

there
but unlocated
lurks the singularity.

Density and utter darkness.
Intensity of undoing

into which a / perhaps / first star
collapsed

and the mind knows—

in queerest ecstasy—

nothing!

Mind Working World

what concerns the artist is that the thing exists—
and he starts with a ruined language
                              —George Oppen

swim through the tangled drift
and

pull out treasures

objects of clarity that
hold the strains   the stains

unashamedly

Method in a Puzzle of Months

Pull from the Great Dictionary
in a game of blindfold bluff
(very English, very old)
played in the wide sky
one word.

Or as if opening the
family Bible, plunk down a single
finger—use a table, have a chair—
into a good book. Any good book.
Begin reading what is written
(in language both venerable and familiar)
from that single point.

The given exists. Stay there. Wait.

Comes then your own small thought.
Hold it. Nurse it. Lay it in its crib.
Overnight it grows, an inevitable
originality emerging, a substantial joy. Which exists.

Do not stay there. Do not wait. Pull again.
Or plunk. Forget delicacy.
Later, though, approach on tiptoe, silent.
See how the little thing sleeps. See how it wakes.

Language Arrives

like scarves pulled
from apparently empty
panhandler's hat,

hat come shyly before floodlights
riding plain brown head of improbable
bewildered magician to whom trick *happens*

as big bum's shoes,
clownish, remain angled, Chaplinesque,
nailed to stage after audience leaves.

The Progress of Thought

In the great matrix of woven sticks
and assorted bits,

accidental thorns
and soft spun cushioning

we (with our tiny bird beaks
open and complaining) fed,

then left the edge and—
first fall reversed,

early wings working,
but the nest not forgotten,

how it held and restricted—
flew.

And daily with difference
comes the great repetition—

falling and flight,
tangle and temptation,

nests everywhere.

The Wild Reality of Time

Is it sad then
or finally right
to hunker down
inside the complex cube,

the home,

where infinity
and her old pal eternity
paint every third wall
a tame shade?

> *(how consistently they arrive at work when expected*
> *in spattered overalls with brushes in hand*
> *and those ladders*
> *and never leave*
>
> *this is quite satisfying is it not*
> *yes it is*
> *yes)*

Do the unpainted others,
walls angled against the dimensions,
breathe while awaiting attention?

Pair

i.
As if they are made of water,
tinted, held, upright, shaped,

thickened, for this is not about flow,
two beings, somewhat removed from gravity,

somewhat still, firmly placed, face one another.
Not an aspect of either is allowed to escape.

Note how they are large, how they are small,
how size in this place lacking background

cannot be known. Inside a child's hand
put these two. Over a city let them hover,

great signs in the sky. But return them
to where nothing else is. They are best there.

How they tremble, for I am their god
and I have banished time.

They must face one another, entire.
Helpless, they must make hearts.

You would give them again the tenderness of the child,
again fling them skyward for glory. Think, though,

how cruel the young human hand can become,
how harmful the high sky turning to storm.

Let us keep them for now in terrified stasis,
unsure how a heart comes to be.

ii.
That watery nature, that slight sea-tint—
shared condition—poor pair!

Where is the required robustness?
Where the wind-whipped complexion?

Denied: a good face to put on their plight.
Denied: all but barest being.

Waiting—even waiting—has been taken away.
I am a crueler god than I knew.

How are they to proceed? Timeless, condemned,
they can use their dark eyes, face each other, gaze.

You, stranger, overlooked the ocular, absorbed in pity.
But I question myself. Does vision escape the stricture?

Slide free from paralysis, become?
Ah, no. The eyes are eternal.

I forgot that fact myself, absent-minded.
No god is perfect; no god, demanding,

keeps tabs on all details.
The posture, the stern pose of godhead, distracts.

Now: we have their dark eyes, the gaze, the ray,
the very beam of two souls, solid as polished wood,

but no gymnast balanced on the beam, no stunned audience.
A pair alone. Heartless and contextless. Alone—

except for their solitary god and, apparently, you.
Who *are* you?

iii.
What is solid is what is between. Will they notice?
Quivering, will they care?

Leave them.
Let's walk a bit, you and I.

I agree, it is good, the green earth, proliferation.
I hadn't expected springtime. I see that you had.

And time itself, the tease of it, the frank possibility: good, too.
So we change places, they and I. I walk their well-used earth.

You might be right to raise the question. Lacking hearts,
they intrigue. Successful, *would* they bore me?

But that was the experiment: whether heart-making
might burst boredom, burst—everything;

whether, with specificity removed, rags of relief proscribed,
it might appear, new at the crux: clash of essence, existence,

clash and tangle, explosion—silent, and sure.
I wanted them again out of nothing—wanted them—

I hadn't expected a companion, nor to dabble in the past tense.
That was the point: no past tense. Stop that grin.

And, yes, this, exactly this, is continuous, fresh, engaging.
But the pair was mired. I thought—

iv.
So there they are, still, beaming their unchanged exchange.
Still watery, heartless, bewildered.

But, wait—do you suppose they know—
that we are here, and for the moment female?

A surprise to me, yes, yes—
you and I! Female!

As they would be if—
As they were and will be.

It wasn't my best idea, dividing the living by sex.
You knew that.

For eons I ignored—such a silly detail—
I sat back, supremely ungendered. Occasionally I sighed.

The texture of existence changes, gendered.
Gendered texture invites. Invitation implies heart.

A tantalizing line of argument, but flawed by fact.
Nevertheless, might you like to dance?

v.
So they knew all along, held to themselves,
allowed no escape, that we came and went—

and came again, two old ladies inclined to waltz.
The giggles that slipped from their wet souls!

Ha! Heart—they knew—is a patient organ,
humble to the point of invisibility,

ingrained in the flimsiest existent,
quite happy to drift suspended in sea-tint,

hiding from an unhappy god. You knew all along.
Stranger, who *are* you?

White Sand Is Most in Repute at Present—
The title is from a publicbookshelf.com article on glassmaking.

On Curved Earth—
"Clarity, clarity...limiting clarity" is from Oppen's "Route";
Samson's roaring and night's boast come from Elisabeth
Murawski's "Zorba's Daughter."

Cast Away the Little Birds—
Derived through erasure from Robert Duncan's "My Mother
Would Be a Falconress."

Dark Myth Left Empty—
The epigraph is from Rilke's *The Notebooks of Malte Laurids
Brigge*. It refers to Goethe, and the limits he placed on contact
with Bettina von Arnim, the young writer obsessed with him.
The lines "spreading out whole..." are drawn from Malte Laurids'
description of Bettina in the same novel. See Stephen Mitchell's
translation, 1990 Vintage International Edition, pages 205-207.

Grinding the Lens—
The epigraph is from Bidart's *Metaphysical Dog*; the poet being
addressed is Walt Whitman.

To See Crimson Roses—
Derived through erasure from Christina Diebold's
"Transformations," with a nod to William Blake.

Out of Nyx—
Derived through erasure from Hesiod's *Theogony*, lines 736-766

Emblem of Appetite—
Derived through erasure from Christina Diebold's "Indra's Net."

Stagecraft in Red (Justice)—

>The card referred to is a tarot card. A coif is a fitted garment covering the hair and neck.

Tension—

>Derived through erasure from Margot Kelley's "Surface Tension."

Near a White Rabbit—

>Derived through erasure from Susan Morse's "Evening Stroll with the Moon Goddess."

The Work—

>"time to fly..." is from Anne Carson's *Decreation*.

Complications of Desire—

>"They flee from us..." is based on a line from Sir Thomas Wyatt; "Nothing is so mute..." is from Rainer Maria Rilke.

About the Author

Shirley Glubka is the author of *Green Surprise of Passion: Writings of a Trauma Therapist*; and *All the Difference: poems of unconventional motherhood*; and *Return to a Meadow*, a novel. She was born in Washington, D.C. in 1942. She is a retired psychotherapist and lives in Prospect, Maine with her spouse, Virginia Holmes.

Shirley's poetry and prose have appeared in such journals as *2River View, Conditions, Feminist Studies, h.o.m.e. Words, Narramissic Notebook, Puckerbrush Review, Seems, Sinister Wisdom,* and *Sun Dog: the Southeast Review*; and in these collections: *Lesbians at Mid-life: the Creative Transition*; and *Mothers Who Leave: the myth of women without their children*; and *Women in Culture: a Women's Studies Anthology*; and, under the name Shirley Starkweather, *Naming: poems by 8 women.*

www.ingramcontent.com/pod-product-compliance
Lightning Source LLC
Chambersburg PA
CBHW061734020426
42331CB00006B/1238